Bible First™

THEN SAID JESUS…, IF YE CONTINUE IN MY WORD,
THEN ARE YE MY DISCIPLES INDEED;

AND YE SHALL KNOW THE TRUTH,
AND THE TRUTH SHALL MAKE YOU FREE.

JOHN 8:31–32

Bible First – Volume 1: Lessons 1-3
Copyright © 2016 by Euro Team Outreach, Inc.

Authors: Joshua Steele, Kelsie Steele, and Teresa Beal

www.getbiblefirst.com

All Scripture quotations are taken from the King James Bible.

First printing: March 2016
Second printing: March 2017
ISBN Print: 978-1-944679-00-2
ISBN eBook: 978-1-944679-06-4
ISBN ePDF: 978-1-944679-12-5
Library of Congress Control Number: 2016931523

1. Genesis; 2. Creation; 3. Manuscript Evidence; 4. Jesus Christ; 5. Trinity; 6. Angels
I. Steele, Joshua; Steele, Kelsie; Beal, Teresa
II. Bible First – Volume 1: Lessons 1-3

Bible First – Volume 1: Lessons 1-3 may be purchased at special quantity discounts. Resale opportunities are available for sales promotions, corporate programs, gifts, fund raising, book clubs, or educational purposes for churches, congregations, schools and universities. For more information contact Mel Cohen:
mel@euroteamoutreach.org
1000 Pearl Road
Pleasantville, TN 37033
931-593-2484

Editors: Nathan Day, Katelin Day, Jessie Beal
Cover design: Joshua Steele
Interior layout: Joshua Steele
Publishing Consultant: Mel Cohen of Inspired Authors Press LLC
www.inspiredauthorspress.com

Printed in the United States of America

Contents

Also available in this series:

Bible First – Volume 2: Lessons 4-6

Bible First – Volume 3: Lessons 7-10

Bible First – Volume 4: Lessons 11-13

Bible First – Volume 5: Lessons 14-17

Bible First – Volume 6: Lessons 18-20

Foreword

Bible First was born in response to a need. In 2004, a small group of independent missionaries came together in western Ukraine to form a ministry known as Euro Team Outreach. Our primary objective was to communicate the Gospel of Jesus Christ to the Ukrainian people. As we searched for ways to do that effectively, we decided to launch a distance-learning course with the stated goal of encouraging people to read the Bible. It was our belief then – and still is today – that the Scriptures themselves represent the single most powerful witness of Christ on earth. To engage a sinner in reading God's Word is to dramatically increase his chances of believing on Christ for salvation. "So then faith cometh by hearing, and hearing by the word of God." (Romans 10:17)

Not finding any existing materials that fit our needs, we decided to write our own course. Our editing team, as we came to call it, included myself and my wife Kelsie, Jessie and Teresa Beal, and Nathan and Katelin Day. Though writing an entire Bible course from scratch was an ambitious goal, our approach was pragmatic. Certain of us drafted new material, and when significant portions were completed, the whole group would convene for editing meetings. Month after month we wrote, edited, rewrote and refined our work, striving to present the message of the Bible in a clear and engaging fashion.

The first lessons were mailed out in 2006 to Ukrainian students who enrolled in response to paper invitations. Soon our list of registered students began to grow, and we found it difficult to produce new material quickly enough to meet the demand. Authoring original curriculum is no easy task, and our efforts were further complicated by the fact that each of us had other ministry responsibilities outside of lesson writing. Additionally, every lesson we finished had to be translated into Ukrainian. Once a translation was complete, Nathan and I would read every word both in Ukrainian and English, meticulously comparing each line and requesting corrections from our translator when needed.

Months stretched into years, and still we kept writing. Every time we produced a new lesson for the course, there were already dozens of students waiting for it. I must confess there were days when I wondered if this task we had undertaken would ever be completed! Yet despite my wavering faith, God blessed our work, and *Bible First* continued to grow. Each summer, we conducted literature campaigns, expanding our reach to new cities and villages across Ukraine.

In time, we discovered that the back-and-forth nature of distance-learning provided an excellent context to communicate the Gospel and introduce people to studying Scripture for themselves. It also opened the door to true discipleship as existing *Bible First* students began to invite their friends to sign up. I still remember how thrilled I was one day when, as I studied some of our enrollment statistics, I realized that over 40% of our students were enrolling via word-of-mouth invitations from existing students!

The twentieth and final lesson of *Bible First* was completed in May of 2014. Since that time, we have seen a steady stream of Ukrainians graduating from the course, and many have expressed interest in becoming *Bible First* coaches themselves.

Our *Bible First* story would not be complete without acknowledging the efforts of Denise Hutchison. Denise joined ETO in 2009, and has worked tirelessly sending and receiving lessons, answering letters, and packaging up various books and Bibles to mail to our Ukrainian students. Over the years, her diligence in maintaining the day-to-day operations of *Bible First* allowed our editing team the time needed to create and refine new material.

Today, *Bible First* in Ukraine reaches students in every one of the country's 24 oblasts. Ukrainians are studying the Scriptures in big cities and small villages, at home, at school, and even from prison. Now, with the publication of *Bible First* in English, people in the United States and around the world can read these lessons for themselves and use them as a platform to point others to the Lord.

Bible First was created to encourage you, dear reader, to search the Scriptures. God has written and preserved His Holy Word, the Bible, so that every individual could have the opportunity to know Him. As you read what we have written in these lessons, may you be moved to read what *He* has written in the Bible. In John 20:31, the Apostle John reminds us: "…these are written, that ye might believe that Jesus is the Christ, the Son of God; and that believing ye might have life through his name."

Joshua Steele
L'viv, Ukraine
February 2016

The ETO Family
From the left: Denise, Jessie, Teresa, Katelin, Nathan, Kelsie, Joshua and Patricia

www.euroteamoutreach.org

About Q&A Booklets

At the conclusion of each *Bible First* lesson, you will be asked to answer a series of questions about the material covered in that lesson. You may write your answers directly in this book or download a printable Q&A booklet from our web site. Answer keys and other supplemental materials are also available. All downloads are provided free of charge.

www.getbiblefirst.com/downloads

How to Become a Coach

Bible First was designed as a platform for evangelism. In addition to the lessons themselves, we have created a variety of training materials and downloadable resources intended to help you launch your own ministry using the *Bible First* program.

To learn more about how you can become a *Bible First* coach, please visit us online at:

www.getbiblefirst.com/training

Need help?

If you have any questions about *Bible First*, you are welcome to contact us directly.

www.getbiblefirst.com/contact

Bible First™

Introducing the Bible

How to complete this lesson

1. Read the lesson.
As you read, be sure to jot down any comments or questions you have. You'll want to keep your King James Bible handy to look up passages as you progress.

2. Answer the questions.
You'll find these in the Q&A section at the end of the lesson. We recommend that you write your answers in the corresponding Q&A booklet* which you may download from our web site.

3. Check your work.
Once you have completed the Q&A booklet, verify your answers with those found in the answer key* for this lesson.

Studying with a coach?
If you were given this book by a Bible First coach, be sure to let them know once you complete this lesson. That way, you can share your work from the Q&A section and discuss what you've learned before continuing to the next lesson.

*Available at www.getbiblefirst.com/downloads

Lesson Overview

- The Bible's Authorship
- The Bible's Preservation
- The Bible's Survival
- The Bible's Contents
- The Bible Is for Us

Introduction

"Blessed are they that hear the word of God, and keep it." (Luke 11:28) The word "Bible" comes from the Greek word "biblios" and simply means, "the book." The Bible has been referred to as "the book of books." As God's Word, it stands far above every other written work and does not require a title. It is enough to call it "The Book."

Of all the literature in the world, the Bible is the most widely circulated and the most extensively translated. It has withstood persecution more than any other book, and after thousands of years continues to be a number one best-seller. The Bible has been better preserved and substantiated than any other ancient document. Its facts have been repeatedly confirmed both historically and archeologically, and the wisdom of its principles have stood the test of time. A book that is so set apart warrants our attention and further investigation.

God is the Author of the Bible

"For this cause also thank we God without ceasing, because, when ye received the word of God which ye heard of us, ye received it not as the word of men, but as it is in truth, the word of God, which effectually worketh also in you that believe." (1 Thessalonians 2:13)

God is the exclusive Author of the Bible, and every word therein is inspired by Him. He chose forty men as instruments to record His words to mankind. These writers of the Bible were men of varying social rank, including kings, scholars, shepherds, peasants, and fishermen, to name a few. They lived at completely different times and in different places, writing from Asia, Africa, and Europe.

The Apostle John pens the book of Revelation on the Isle of Patmos.

Most people would be amazed to know that the authorship of the Bible took place over a period of 1600 years, spanning 40 generations. The Old Testament was written in Hebrew and Aramaic, while Greek was the language of the New Testament. With such disparity of authorship, languages, cultures, and times, one would expect to find a disjointed collection of philosophies and fables, or at best, a compilation of feeble moral teachings. However, in examining the Bible we find the exact opposite to be true: its message is consistent and unified, with each book building logically on the one before it. Its 40 writers wrote with remarkable agreement despite the hundreds or even thousands of years separating their lives. The Bible explains this uniformity: *"...Prophecy came not in old time by the will of man: but holy men of God spake as they were moved by the Holy Ghost." (2 Peter 1:21)*

When God authored the Bible, He communicated to the men He had chosen in three different ways:

- He spoke to them audibly.
- He spoke to them in visions.
- He put the message directly into their minds.

Some, like Moses and Job, heard God speaking to them, while Daniel and Ezekiel saw prophecies of things to come in dreams and visions. The entire Book of Revelation was written by the Apostle John as a result of his vision on the Isle of Patmos. Other books, like the Pauline epistles, were written as letters to the early churches by the Apostle Paul. The gospels were recorded from the experiences of men like Matthew, John, and others who walked with Jesus and talked with Him face to face.

Regardless of how the message was communicated, the words that these men wrote in the Bible were inspired by God. 2 Timothy 3:16-17 tells us, *"All Scripture is given by inspiration of God and is profitable for doctrine, for reproof, for correction, for instruction in righteousness, that the man of God may be perfect, throughly furnished unto all good works."*

As Lewis S. Chafer, founder and former president of the Dallas Theological Seminary said, "The Bible is not such a book a man would write if he could, or could write if he would."

Preservation of the Old Testament

"Forever, O LORD, thy word is settled in heaven." (Psalm 119:89) God first entrusted His Word to the Jewish nation, with the intent that they would proclaim its message throughout the world. They were extremely proud of this inheritance and zealously protected the authenticity of every word, at times even sacrificing their lives for the preservation of the Scriptures.

Over the centuries, the Jews chose out men known as scribes who were expert in copying and preserving the Word of God. They were highly trained professionals who adhered to a system of precise checks and balances. Two prominent groups dedicated to replicating the Scriptures, the Talmudists and the Massoretes, stand out in the annals of history, and provide an accurate depiction of the extreme delicacy and care with which the Word of God was handled and passed down to each succeeding generation.

The following list of disciplines were practiced by the Talmudists when transcribing the Scriptures:[1]

1. A synagogue roll must be written on the skins of clean animals. (Specified in Leviticus 11)

2. A synagogue roll must be prepared for particular use by a Jew.

3. Synagogue rolls must be fastened together with strings taken from clean animals.

4. Every skin must contain a certain number of columns, equal throughout the entire codex.[2]

5. The length of each column must not extend over less than 48 or more than 60 lines; and the breadth must consist of

---

1. Samuel Davidson, *Hebrew Text of the Old Testament, 2nd edition,* London, Samuel Bagster & Sons, 1859

2. an ancient manuscript text in book form.

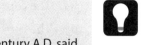

Did you know?

Josephus, famous Jewish historian of the first century A.D. said, "We have given practical proof of our reverence for our own Scriptures. For, although such long ages have now passed, no one has ventured either to add, or to remove, or to alter a syllable; and it is an instinct with every Jew…to regard them as the decrees of God."

thirty letters.

6. The whole copy must first be lined; and if three words be written without a line, it is worthless.

7. The ink should be black; neither red, green, nor any other color, and be prepared according to a definite recipe.

8. An authentic copy must be the exemplar, from which the transcriber ought not in the least to deviate.

9. No word or letter, not even a yod (tenth letter of the Hebrew alphabet), must be written from memory, the scribe not having looked at the codex before him.

10. Between every consonant the space of a hair or thread must intervene.

11. Between every new parashah, or section, there must be the breadth of nine consonants.

12. Between every book, there must be three lines.

13. The fifth book of Moses must terminate exactly with a line; but the rest need not do so.

14. The copyist must first wash his whole body.

15. The copyist must sit in full Jewish dress.

16. The copyist may not begin to write the name of God with a pen newly dipped in ink. (This ensured that God's name was never written with a blot.)

17. While writing the name of God, the copyist should take no notice even if he is addressed by a king.

18. The rolls in which these regulations are not observed are condemned to be buried in the ground or burned.

The Bible Says

"The words of the LORD are pure words: as silver tried in a furnace of earth, purified seven times. Thou shalt keep them, O LORD, thou shalt preserve them from this generation for ever." (Psalm 12: 6-7)

"The same extreme care which was devoted to the transcription of manuscripts is also at the bottom of the disappearance of the earlier copies. When a manuscript had been copied with the exactitude prescribed by the Talmud, and had been duly verified, it was accepted as authentic and regarded as being of equal value with any other copy. If all were equally correct, age gave no advantage to a manuscript; on the contrary, age was a positive disadvantage, since a manuscript was liable to become defaced or damaged in the lapse of time. A damaged or imperfect copy was at once condemned as unfit for use."[3]

Like the Talmudists, the Massoretes were also very stringent in their dealings with the Scriptures. They handled them "with the greatest imaginable reverence, and devised a complicated system of safeguards against scribal slips. They counted, for example, the number of times each letter of the alphabet occurs in each book; they pointed out the middle letter of the Pentateuch and

---

3. Frederic G. Kenyon, *Our Bible and the Ancient Manuscripts*, Kessinger Publishing, LLC, July 2007

The Accuracy of the New Testament

"There is no body of ancient literature in the world which enjoys such a wealth of good textual attestation as the New Testament."[6]

The New Testament is substantiated by an overwhelming amount of evidence. Today, over 24,000 partial and complete ancient manuscript copies of the New Testament exist and are available for examination. When compared to other writings of ancient history, no other document even begins to approach such numbers. For example, only 643 manuscripts of Homer's Iliad remain, and even fewer survive from other authors: 8 copies of Herodotus' writings, 5 from Aristotle, 10 from Caesar, and 7 from Pliny the historian. The average ancient secular work is authenticated by a handful of copies, the New Testament by thousands.

One scholar states, "To be skeptical of the resultant text of the New Testament books is to allow all of classical antiquity to slip into obscurity, for no documents of the ancient period are as well attested bibliographically as the New Testament."[7]

In addition, most works of ancient literature average a disparity of 1000 years between the original composition of the document and the earliest copy in existence. However, the existing manuscript copies of the New Testament are separated from their originals by only 200-250 years, and in some cases by less

Key Concept

God has supernaturally preserved His Word so that none of it has been lost.

---

6. F.F. Bruce, *The Books and Parchments, Revised edition*, Westwood: Fleming H. Revell Co., 1963

7. John W. Montgomery, *History and Christianity*, Downers Grove, IL, Inter-Varsity Press, 1971

than a generation.

Not only is the New Testament substantiated by its own manuscripts, there are also over 86,000 quotations by early church writers to further validate its accuracy. In fact, even if there were no other copies of the Bible in existence, there are enough of these excerpts to reconstruct all but 11 verses of the entire New Testament. The complete Bible could also be reassembled from the works of contemporary writers. "If every Bible in any considerable city were destroyed, the Book could be restored in all its essential parts from the quotations on the shelves of the city public library. There are works, covering almost all the great literary writers, devoted especially to showing how much the Bible has influenced them."[8]

Historical Feature

In 1947, about fifteen miles from Jerusalem, a shepherd boy threw a rock into a cave. He heard the sound of pottery breaking and went inside to investigate. To his amazement, he beheld pottery urns holding ancient scrolls. He reported his find, and when scholars investigated, they found hundreds of scrolls. These "Dead Sea Scrolls" had been hidden in area caves by a religious group called the Essenes sometime during the first century B.C. At the time of this discovery, translators were using manuscripts which had been copied around A.D. 900. When scholars compared the Dead Sea Scrolls with the manuscripts they had been using, there were no significant differences in text. Though separated by 1,000 years, these ancient manuscripts were virtually the same.

---

8. Cleland B. McAfee, *The Greatest English Classic*, New York, 1912

The Bible is Indestructible

"We might as well put our shoulder to the burning wheel of the sun, and try to stop it on its flaming course, as attempt to stop the circulation of the Bible." –Anonymous

Not only has the Bible been the most beloved and sought after Book in the entire world, it has also been the most bitterly opposed. Throughout history, the Bible has undergone and withstood more attacks, persecutions, and attempts at annihilation than any other book. Countless monarchs and governments have tried to obliterate the Scriptures, while persecuting the people who read and believed them. Thousands of copies of the Word of God have been burned in heaps. Indeed, the Bible has been the object of such particular persecution that its survival to the present day is nothing less than a miracle.

The Bible Says

"The counsel of the LORD standeth for ever, the thoughts of his heart to all generations." (Psalm 33:11)

Beginning with Nero, the Roman Emperors aggressively persecuted Christians and the Word of God over a period of 300 years. It is recorded that the Emperor Diocletian slew over 20,000 Christians in his reign alone. At an interim when the remaining Christians were in hiding, he believed he had succeeded in eradicating the Scriptures. Delighted with this accomplishment, he commanded that a medal be made and engraved with these words, "The Christian religion is destroyed and the worship of the gods restored."

Down through the ages, various European monarchs and religious leaders also led vicious attacks on the Word of God and its followers. Among the worst was Mary I of England, (1516-1558) known as "Bloody Mary" because of the great number of Christians who were burned at the stake during her reign. Many other English kings fought against the translation of the

The Bible Says

"The grass withereth, the flower fadeth: but the word of our God shall stand forever." (Isaiah 40:8)

Scriptures into the English language. The French monarchs were also known for their animosity towards the propagation of the Scriptures, instigating organized massacres against the Christian faith that lasted for decades.

During the reign of Henry the VIII, William Tyndale worked arduously to translate the Scriptures into the English language. His earnest desire was that the common people would have the opportunity to hold and read the Word of God in their own tongue. He said, "...if God spares my life, I will cause the boy that drives the plow in England to know more of the Scriptures than the Pope himself!" He spent his life as a fugitive, running from the ever watchful eye of religious leaders who sought to stamp out any attempt to spread of the Word of God. By the time he was apprehended, he had completed his translation of the entire Bible into English, as well as a second revision of his New Testament work. He was tried for his "crimes" and later strangled and burned at the stake. His final words were, "Lord! Open the King of England's eyes." The sacrifice of his life for the Word of God's sake is only one example among hundreds of men who willingly gave their lives for the truth of the Scriptures.

A page from William Tyndale's New Testament

During the early twentieth century, the Soviet government mandated a Communist ideology that denied the existence of God. They attempted to entirely eliminate religion within the Soviet Union. As a result of this, the Bible was prohibited and its followers severely oppressed. In many cases, they were imprisoned, sent to forced labor camps, or killed. Communist countries had strict indictments against possessing a Bible and closed their borders to any kind of religious literature. Nevertheless, such restrictions could not stop the spread of Christianity, and the Scriptures continued to be read and circulated as "illegal literature."

Many countries today governed by Communists, fanatical extremists, or dictatorships still limit or completely suppress the production and circulation of the Bible. Christians are giving their lives for placing faith in the Bible as the supreme Word of God.

The Bible Says

"Thy word is very pure: therefore thy servant loveth it." (Psalm 119:140)

Noted 16th century French philosopher Voltaire once predicted, "One hundred years from my day there will not be a Bible in the earth except one that is looked upon by an antiquarian curiosity seeker." Today however, over four centuries later, portions of the Bible have been translated into nearly 2,500 of the 5,000 languages of the world, exceeding any other book in circulation by a huge margin. Far from being forgotten, the Bible "has led to the overthrow of governments, sparked mass migrations across oceans, and more than once changed the course of history."[9] Attacks against the Bible have only served to strengthen its credibility and further its message. Since the time of the Romans, kings and queens, emperors, governments, religious leaders and political regimes have all tried to destroy this book. Instead, they

---

9. Jay Rogers, *The Book that Changed History*, The Forerunner, December 2007

have passed into historical oblivion, lives forgotten, efforts futile. The Book of books lives on.

The Bible Says

"So mightily grew the word of God and prevailed." (Acts 19:20)

Historical Feature

"It was the nineteenth year of Diocletian's reign [A.D. 303] and the month Dystrus, called March by the Romans, and the festival of the Saviour's Passion was approaching, when an imperial decree was published everywhere, ordering the churches to be razed to the ground and the Scriptures destroyed by fire, and giving notice that those in places of honour would lose their places, and domestic staff, if they continued to profess Christianity, would be deprived of their liberty. Such was the first edict against us. Soon afterwards other decrees arrived in rapid succession, ordering that the presidents of the churches in every place should all be first committed to prison and then coerced by every possible means into offering sacrifice [to the Roman gods]."[10]

---

10. Eusebius, *History of the Church, VIII.2*

The Contents of the Bible

"Thy word is true from the beginning: and every one of thy righteous judgments endureth for ever." (Psalm 119:160) The Bible is composed of two major sections: the Old Testament, and the New Testament.

The Old Testament

The Old Testament tells the story of the creation of the world, the beginning of mankind, and God's dealings with the nation of Israel, chronicling their history up until the time of Christ. God used Israel as a channel to reveal His truth to the world. He spoke to them through prophets and kings, giving them hundreds of prophecies regarding future kingdoms and the coming of a Messiah who would be the Savior of all mankind.

The Old Testament reveals God's mighty power, love, justice, and mercy through story after intriguing story. In it are captivating accounts of fire coming down from heaven, strong men slaying wild animals, kings waging battles and besieging cities, whole armies drowning in the sea or being slain by angels, famines, murders, giants, love affairs, and people being raised from the dead, just to name a few.

The Old Testament contains 39 books which are divided into five categories:

The Books of the Law (5)
- Genesis
- Exodus
- Leviticus
- Numbers
- Deuteronomy

The Historical Books (12)
- Joshua
- Judges
- Ruth
- 1 Samuel
- 2 Samuel
- 1 Kings
- 2 Kings
- 1 Chronicles
- 2 Chronicles

Introducing the Bible   **17**

- Ezra
- Nehemiah
- Esther

The Poetical Books (5)
- Job
- Psalms
- Proverbs
- Ecclesiastes
- Song of Solomon

The Major Prophets (5)
- Isaiah
- Jeremiah
- Lamentations
- Ezekiel
- Daniel

The Minor Prophets (12)
- Hosea
- Joel
- Amos
- Obadiah
- Jonah
- Micah
- Nahum
- Habakkuk
- Zephaniah
- Haggai
- Zechariah
- Malachi

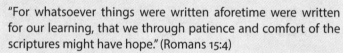

The Bible Says

"For whatsoever things were written aforetime were written for our learning, that we through patience and comfort of the scriptures might have hope." (Romans 15:4)

The New Testament

The central character of the New Testament is Jesus Christ: His time on earth, His message, His followers, and His second coming. The New Testament begins with the account of supernatural events surrounding Jesus Christ's birth, life, death and resurrection. Following His ascension into Heaven, it goes on to tell of the giving of the Holy Spirit, and the establishment of the early church. Courageous followers of Jesus spread His message of forgiveness for sins throughout Israel, Samaria, the Roman Empire, and the world. The New Testament also contains many letters written by Paul or other apostles explaining the doctrines of Christ and instructing believers to live in godliness.

The New Testament contains 27 books, making a total of 66 books in the entire Bible. Its books are divided into five categories:

The Gospels (4)
- Matthew
- Mark
- Luke
- John

History (1)
- Acts

The Pauline Epistles (14)
- Romans
- 1 Corinthians
- 2 Corinthians
- Galatians
- Ephesians
- Philippians
- Colossians
- 1 Thessalonians
- 2 Thessalonians
- 1 Timothy
- 2 Timothy
- Titus
- Philemon
- Hebrews

The General Epistles (7)
- James
- 1 Peter
- 2 Peter
- 1 John
- 2 John
- 3 John
- Jude

Prophecy (1)
- Revelation

Did You Know?

The Bible was divided into chapters by Stephen Langton in the thirteenth century, and into verses in the fifteenth and sixteenth centuries. The first Bible to be printed in the modern chapter-verse format was Stephanus' Latin Bible of 1555.[11]

The Bible Is for Us

The Bible is not a mere collection of truthful sayings, stories, and maxims for life. Unlike other religious books, the Bible is alive. It is powerful and influential. Its words go down into the innermost soul of man and expose the motives of the heart. *"For the word of God is quick [alive], and powerful, and sharper than any twoedged sword, piercing even to the dividing asunder of soul and spirit, and of the joints and marrow, and is a discerner of the thoughts and intents of the heart."* (Hebrews 4:12)

Consider a few examples of how the Word of God is capable of bringing change and affecting our lives.

- It causes us to grow. (1 Peter 2:2)
- It makes us wise unto salvation. (2 Timothy 3:15)
- By it we are cleansed. (John 15:3)
- By it we are defended against spiritual wickedness. (Ephesians 6:17)
- It illuminates our path through life. (Psalm 119:105)
- It causes us to rejoice. (Jeremiah 15:16)
- By it we are warned. (Psalm 19:11)

---

11. David W. Cloud, *Way of Life Encyclopedia of the Bible & Christianity*, Way of Life Literature, Oak Harbor, WA, Oct. 1997

The Bible Says

"Thy word is a lamp unto my feet, and a light unto my path."
(Psalm 119:105)

In addition to the Bible being a living Book, it is our only basis for absolute truth. Apart from it, a person has no authority - no foundation on which to build his ideas, relationships, work, and existence. Knowing the truth of the Bible gives us motivation for life - a security of knowledge and principle from which we can derive a sense of purpose and peace. A life without the Bible's direction, a life without truth, is a meaningless existence.

The Bible is our living link with a God we cannot see. Contrary to what most people think, God is not a remote mystical Being who has little interest in our lives. God loves us and wants for us to fellowship with Him as our Creator, Father, Savior, and Friend.

Key Concept

The Bible is our living link with a God we cannot see.

God has written and preserved His Word for the express purpose of allowing us to know Him and understand His truth. Reading the Bible allows us to have a relationship with God Himself and receive His wisdom for every aspect of our lives, including: finding God's will for us personally, maintaining healthy relationships, experiencing marital success, raising happy and productive children, coping with crises, living in victory over sin, and preparing for death and eternity.

In the Bible, God gives us many invitations to know Him:

- *"Come unto me all ye that labor and are heavy laden..."* *(Matthew 11:28)*
- *"O taste and see that the LORD is good..." (Psalm 34:8)*
- *"...Whosoever will, let him take the water of life freely." (Revelation 22:17)*
- *"Look unto me, and be ye saved, all the ends of the earth: for I am God, and there is none else." (Isaiah 45:22)*

Did You Know?

The Bible gives us many word pictures to help us visualize its power and functions. The Word of God refers to itself as:

- Light (Psalm 43:3, 2 Peter 1:19)
- A hammer (Jeremiah 23:29)
- Fire (Jeremiah 23:29)
- A sword (Hebrews 4:12; Ephesians 6:17)
- A lamp (Psalm 119:105)
- Water (Ephesians 5:26)
- Honey (Psalm 119:103)
- Seed (Luke 8:11; 1 Peter 1:23)
- Milk (1 Peter 2:2)
- Meat (Hebrews 5:12, 14)

Conclusion

Throughout the ages, the Bible has repeatedly proven its reliability and effectiveness. It comes to us from the very mouth of God: pure, preserved, indestructible, complete and powerful. Not only is it historically relevant, but even today influences the course of current events as well as individual lives.

In one small volume, we hold in our hands the key to unlocking the mysteries of divine thought, the means of exploring the depth of the very heart of our Creator, the manual for developing lives of fulfillment and purpose. Yet very often, this amazing book so full of opportunity is ignored, becoming nothing more than a talisman gathering dust on the shelf.

So what should we do with the Bible?

- **Study it:** *"Study to shew thyself approved unto God, a workman that needeth not to be ashamed, rightly dividing the word of truth." (2 Timothy 2:15)*
- **Receive it:** *"Wherefore lay apart all filthiness and superfluity of naughtiness, and receive with meekness the engrafted word, which is able to save your souls." (James 1:21)*
- **Believe it:** *"When therefore he was risen from the dead, his disciples remembered that he had said this unto them; and they believed the scripture, and the word which Jesus had said." (John 2:22)*
- **Obey it:** *"But be ye doers of the word, and not hearers only, deceiving your own selves." (James 1:22)*
- **Memorize it:** *"Thy word have I hid in mine heart, that I might not sin against thee." (Psalm 119:11)*

In the words of well-known British Bible teacher, Charles Haddon Spurgeon:

"This volume is the writing of the living God; each letter was penned with an Almighty finger; each word in it dropped from the everlasting lips; each sentence was dictated by the Holy Spirit. Albeit, that Moses was employed to write his histories with his fiery pen, God guided that pen. It may be that David touched his harp and let sweet Psalms of melody drop from his fingers, but God moved his hands over the living strings of his golden harp. It may be that Solomon sang canticles of love, or gave forth words of consummate wisdom, but God directed his lips and made the preacher eloquent. If I follow the thundering Nahum, when his horses plough the waters, or Habakkuk,

Charles Spurgeon
1834 - 1892

when he sees the tents of Cushan in affliction; if I read Malachi, when the earth is burning like an oven; if I turn to the smooth page of John, who tells of love, or the rugged, fiery chapters of Peter, who speaks of fire devouring God's enemies; if I turn to Jude, who launches forth anathemas upon the foes of God— everywhere I find God speaking. It is God's voice, not man's; the words are God's words, the words of the Eternal, the Invisible, the Almighty, the Jehovah of this earth."[12]

"BLESSED IS THE MAN THAT WALKETH NOT IN THE COUNSEL OF THE UNGODLY, NOR STANDETH IN THE WAY OF SINNERS, NOR SITTETH IN THE SEAT OF THE SCORNFUL.

BUT HIS DELIGHT IS IN THE LAW OF THE LORD; AND IN HIS LAW DOTH HE MEDITATE DAY AND NIGHT.

AND HE SHALL BE LIKE A TREE PLANTED BY THE RIV-ERS OF WATER, THAT BRINGETH FORTH HIS FRUIT IN HIS SEASON; HIS LEAF ALSO SHALL NOT WITHER; AND WHAT-SOEVER HE DOETH SHALL PROSPER."

PSALM 1:1-3

---

12. Sermon delivered by Charles Spurgeon on March 18, 1855 at Exeter Hall, Strand. http://www.spurgeongems.org/vols1-3/chs15.pdf

Before continuing to the next lesson, please answer all the questions in the Q&A section below. If you prefer, you can download a printable Q&A booklet and answer key from our web site:

www.getbiblefirst.com/downloads

1. What is the meaning of the word "Bible"?

   _____

2. Fill in the blank. God is the exclusive Author of the Bible and every word therein is _____ by Him.

3. How many men were chosen as instruments to record God's words to mankind?

   _____

4. Fill in the blanks. The Bible was written over a period of _____ years, spanning _____ generations.

5. Name the three languages in which the Bible was written.

   1. _____

2. _____

3. _____

6. Name the three ways God communicated to the men who wrote the Bible.

   1. _____

   2. _____

   3. _____

7. The Bible tells us in 2 Timothy 3: 16-17, "All Scripture is given by inspiration of God and is profitable

   for _____,

   for _____,

   for _____,

   for _____,

   that the man of God may be perfect, throughly furnished unto all good works."

8. Name the two prominent groups that were dedicated to replicating the Scriptures.

   1. _____

   2. _____

9. The discovery of which ancient scrolls supported the accuracy of the Scriptures?

   _____

10. Explain why age was a disadvantage to a manuscript document.

    _____

    _____

    _____

11. Define manuscript evidence.

    _____

    _____

    _____

12. How many copies of ancient manuscripts have survived for each of the following:

    ❑ Homer's Iliad: _____

    ❑ Herodotus' writings: _____

    ❑ Aristotle: _____

    ❑ Caesar: _____

    ❑ Pliny: _____

    ❑ The New Testament: _____

13. Fill in the blank. The Bible's survival to the present day is nothing less than a _____.

14. Who gave his life so that the common people of England could read the Word of God in their own language?

    _____

15. The Bible is composed of what two major sections?

    _____

16. How is the Bible different from other religious books? (choose one)
    - ❑ It's longer
    - ❑ It's older
    - ❑ It's alive
    - ❑ It has interesting stories and good principles

17. Fill in the blanks. "For the word of God is

    _____, and _____,

    and _____ than any twoedged sword,

    piercing even to the dividing asunder of soul and spirit,

    and of the joints and marrow, and is a _____

    _____."

    Hebrews 4:12

18. Name at least three ways in which the Bible is capable of bringing change and affecting our lives.

    1. _____

    2. _____

    3. _____

19. What draws us to have a relationship with God Himself and receive His wisdom for every aspect of our lives?

    _____

20. What five things should we do with the Bible?

    1. _____

    2. _____

    3. _____

    4. _____

    5. _____

Lesson 2

Bible First™

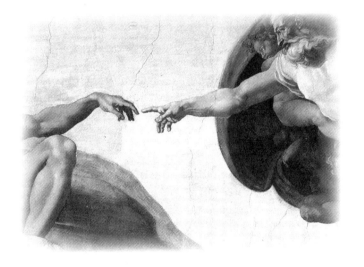

Who is God?

How to complete this lesson

1. Read the lesson.
As you read, be sure to jot down any comments or questions you have. You'll want to keep your King James Bible handy to look up passages as you progress.

2. Answer the questions.
You'll find these in the Q&A section at the end of the lesson. We recommend that you write your answers in the corresponding Q&A booklet* which you may download from our web site.

3. Check your work.
Once you have completed the Q&A booklet, verify your answers with those found in the answer key* for this lesson.

Studying with a coach?
If you were given this book by a Bible First coach, be sure to let them know once you complete this lesson. That way, you can share your work from the Q&A section and discuss what you've learned before continuing to the next lesson.

*Available at www.getbiblefirst.com/downloads

Lesson Overview

- The Attributes of God
- The Character of God
- God in Three Persons

Introduction

The primary goal of the Bible is to introduce the reader to the Author. God Almighty, the Creator of all that is, desires that we would have a personal relationship with Him. In order for us to know Him, God has provided an accurate picture of who He is in the Bible. Although it is impossible to thoroughly explore God in only one lesson, this study will provide a general introduction to God's nature.

Key Concept

No man has ever seen God, nor can our finite minds fully comprehend Him.

The Primary Attributes of God

The Apostle Paul made this observation in his epistle to the Romans when he exclaimed, *"O the depth of the riches both of the wisdom and knowledge of God! how unsearchable are his judgments, and his ways past finding out! For who hath known the mind of the Lord? or who hath been his counsellor? Or who hath first given to him, and it shall be recompensed unto him again? For of him, and through him, and to him, are all things: to whom be glory for ever. Amen."* *(Romans 11:33-36)* God is greater in wisdom and power than the human mind can comprehend. He is not limited to the rules of nature that govern all of mankind. Although one can walk with God for years and not even approach the limits of His greatness, the following is a look at His chief qualities and attributes.

The Bible Says

"Great is our Lord, and of great power: his understanding is infinite." (Psalm 147:5)

God is All-knowing

Men have been studying for thousands of years and still have not exhausted the realm of scientific learning. New discoveries are made daily in regard to the human body, the universe, and the elements. As the Creator, only God has perfect, unlimited knowledge of all things. He has no need to reason or acquire learning, as in the case of men. God's knowledge is innate, intuitive, and eternal. The Bible tells us in Psalm 147:5, *"Great is our Lord, and of great power: his understanding is infinite."* Nothing can be hidden from His sight, nothing is new or surprising to Him. *"Neither is there any creature that is not manifest in his sight: but all things are naked and opened unto the eyes of him with whom we have to do."* *(Hebrews 4:13)*

Not only did God engineer the wonders of the universe, He also masterminded the intricacies of the human make-up. He has great personal interest in each individual life. King David recognized God's intimate knowledge of his life when he wrote, *"Thou knowest mine downsitting and mine uprising, thou understandest my thought afar off. Thou compassest my path and my lying down, and art acquainted with all my ways." (Psalm 139:2-3)* God knows our past, our present, and our future. He sees our lives and actions and knows the very thoughts of our heart.

God is All-powerful

In Jeremiah 32:17 we read, *"Ah Lord God! behold, thou hast made the heaven and the earth by thy great power and stretched out arm, and there is nothing too hard for thee:"* God's works are effortless. He upholds all things without the force of labor associated with human exertion. He does not tire or become weary. God rules over all things:

- All nature is subject to His will and command. *"The earth is the LORD'S, and the fulness thereof; the world, and they that dwell therein. For he hath founded it upon the seas, and established it upon the floods." (Psalm 24:1-2)*

- God's power prevails over men and nations. *"...O LORD God of our fathers, art not thou God in heaven? and rulest not thou over all the kingdoms of the heathen? and in thine hand is there not power and might, so that none is able to withstand thee?" (2 Chronicles 20:6)*

- All angels recognize His authority. *"Bless the LORD, ye*

his angels, that excel in strength, that do his commandments, hearkening unto the voice of his word." (Psalm 103:20)

- All satanic hosts acknowledge His power. *"Thou believest that there is one God; thou doest well: the devils also believe, and tremble." (James 2:19)*

Is there anything God cannot do? The Scriptures clearly show the answer to be yes. God cannot sin, God cannot lie, God cannot deny Himself, God cannot change or act contrary to His nature. (Numbers 23:19; 2 Timothy 2:13; James 1:13,17; 1 John 1:5) However, when the Bible speaks of God's power, there is no end or limit to what He can do. The word "impossible" is not in God's vocabulary. Nonetheless, God's power is never used for evil or selfish designs; rather it always works in accord with His wisdom and goodness.

Key Concept

All things are possible with God.

God is All-present

"God, the Creator and Sustainer of all things is present universally and simultaneously in every part of His wide domain, and is able to put forth His entire power in every place at one and the same time."[1]

God is an eyewitness in every geographical location and to every circumstance and event. *"The eyes of the LORD are in every place, beholding the evil and the good." (Proverbs 15:3)* His presence fills the earth, the heavens, and the whole universe. No place is exempt from the perception, awareness, and being of Almighty God. Man, angels, and even Satan are limited by distance and space, but God exists outside the "rules of nature". He created the rules. *"Can any hide himself in secret places that I shall not see him? saith the LORD. Do not I fill heaven and earth? saith the LORD." (Jeremiah 23:24)*

---

1. Herbert Lockyer, *All the Doctrines of the Bible*, Grand Rapids, MI, 1964

God is Holy

In Exodus 15:11, we read, *"Who is like unto thee, O LORD, among the gods? who is like thee, glorious in holiness, fearful in praises, doing wonders?"* God is absolutely holy. This fact greatly distinguishes God from all of His creation. Holiness is not merely another part of His character, rather it is His very essence.

The holiness of God is such that it is constantly proclaimed before His presence. Angelic beings before God's throne cry without ceasing, *"...Holy, holy, holy, Lord God Almighty, which was, and is, and is to come." (Revelation 4:8, see also Isaiah 6:3)* Even the holiest of men and angels cannot begin to attain to the holiness of God. As the origin and source of all holiness, God stands as its ultimate zenith. The Bible tells us that the few who have stood before God Himself have been completely overwhelmed and cannot but recognize the enormity of their own uncleanness.

"Then said I [the prophet Isaiah], Woe is me! for I am undone;

because I am a man of unclean lips...for mine eyes have seen the King, the LORD of hosts." (Isaiah 6:5)

"And when I [the Apostle John] saw him, I fell at his feet as dead. And he laid his right hand upon me, saying unto me, Fear not; I am the first and the last: I am he that liveth, and was dead; and, behold, I am alive for evermore, Amen; and have the keys of hell and of death." (Revelation 1:17-18)

Because God loves holiness, His very being loathes sin and cannot allow it to abide in His presence. He is completely pure and clean, incapable of acting unrighteously or tempting others to sin. Holiness governs all of God's dealings with man, and His attitude toward sin will always be to condemn it.

God is Love

The one attribute of God which is most universally recognized and spoken of is love. The Bible tells us in I John 4:8, *"...God is love."* God's love, as defined in 1 Corinthians 13, is unselfish, kind, longsuffering, seeking the good of another, and promoting truth and righteousness.

"Charity suffereth long, and is kind; charity envieth not; charity vaunteth not itself, is not puffed up, Doth not behave itself unseemly, seeketh not her own, is not easily provoked, thinketh no evil; Rejoiceth not in iniquity, but rejoiceth in the truth; Beareth all things, believeth all things, hopeth all things, endureth all things." (1 Corinthians 13:4-7)

God's love is manifested in many ways. He cares for the wants, concerns, behaviors, and instincts of all His creation, providing air, food, and shelter to even the lowest order of animals. To man, God has given the whole earth and all its resources for sustenance, development, and productivity. Such a gift not only satisfies man's physical needs, but also fulfills his intellectual and emotional drives to create, produce, invent, raise, and conquer. God's love has further lavished upon man the gifts of life, health, family, marriage, and friendship for his enjoyment.

"Blessed be the Lord, who daily loadeth us with benefits, even the God of our salvation. Selah." (Psalm 68:19)

The love of God prompts Him to declare Himself the Father of those who trust and obey Him. To such He extends favor, blessings, and provision for their needs. To the sinner, God manifests longsuffering and forbearance, leading them to repentance. (Romans 2:4) He offers full forgiveness and cleansing from sin, turning once corrupted men and women into sons and daughters of His kingdom.

The Bible Explored

It was the custom in Old Testament times for a person to outline or trace on the palm of his hand the name of his god or any object of love. This engraving was a constant reminder to him of his loved ones. God, in order to illustrate the strength and permanency of His love toward the people of Israel, made this statement in Isaiah 49:15-16, *"Can a woman forget her sucking child, that she should not have compassion on the son of her womb? yea, they may forget, yet will I not forget thee [Israel]. Behold, I have graven thee upon the palms of my hands...."* God is always mindful of those He loves.

God is Just

Although God is perfect in His love, He is absolutely just and righteous in His dealings with man. His love does not deter Him from upholding and defending righteousness, or from punishing sin. He acts fairly with all men, loving the things that are good and hating the things that are evil.

"But let him that glorieth glory in this, that he understandeth and knoweth me, that I am the LORD which exercise lovingkindness, judgment, and righteousness, in the earth: for in these things I delight, saith the LORD." (Jeremiah 9:24)

God's justice rewards men equitably according to their works. He holds all to one standard of righteousness; He cannot be swayed, manipulated or influenced. He does not exercise His power randomly or with discrimination. Rather, He is the Just Judge of all mankind, rewarding the righteous for their good deeds and punishing the wicked for their sin.

"If thou sayest, Behold, we knew it not; doth not he [God] that pondereth the heart consider it ? and he that keepeth thy soul, doth not he know it? and shall not he render to every man according to his works?" (Proverbs 24:12)

Even when we do not understand the suffering and injustice around us, it is important to realize that these are the result of man's rebellion against his Maker. God Himself remains just and will ultimately avenge the afflicted. In the words of Herbert Lockyer, "In this we rest that God knows what is right and that because of His justice, sin which He hates must be punished sometime, somewhere; and that all life's suffering and seeming inequalities will be rightly adjusted."[2]

Key Concept

God loves righteousness and hates sin.

The Bible Says

"Touching the Almighty, we cannot find him out: he is excellent in power, and in judgment, and in plenty of justice: he will not afflict." (Job 37:23)

---

2. Herbert Lockyer, *All the Doctrines of the Bible*, Grand Rapids, MI, 1964

The Trinity

The Bible tells us that there is ONE God, but that He is THREE persons. This concept is called the doctrine of the Trinity. *"For there are three that bear record in heaven, the Father, the Word, and the Holy Ghost: and these three are one."* (1 John 5:7) Although God is three distinct persons, Scripture clearly describes them as co-equal.

Although the actual word *trinity* is not found in the Bible, the teaching of the Trinity is undeniably a Scriptural truth. Following are some instances in Scripture which establish God's three-fold nature:

- Jesus is baptized: *"And Jesus, when he was baptized, went up straightway out of the water: and, lo, the heavens were opened unto him, and he saw the Spirit of God descending like a dove, and lighting upon him: And lo a voice from heaven [the Father], saying, This is my beloved Son, in whom I am well pleased."* (Matthew 3:16-17)

- Jesus teaches His disciples: *"But the Comforter, which is the Holy Ghost, whom the Father will send in my name [the Son], he shall teach you all things, and bring all things to your remembrance, whatsoever I have said unto you."* (John 14:26)

- Jesus commands His disciples: *"Go ye therefore, and teach all nations, baptizing them in the name of the Father, and of the Son, and of the Holy Ghost:"* (Matthew 28:19)

- Paul blesses the Corinthian church in the name of all three: *"The grace of the Lord Jesus Christ, and the love of God, and the communion of the Holy Ghost, be with you all. Amen."* (2 Corinthians 13:14)

The New Testament proclaims a Father who is God, a Son who is God, and a Holy Spirit who is God, each one manifesting the

Godhead in all of its fullness.

God the Father:
- *"...Grace to you and peace from God our Father, and the Lord Jesus Christ." (Romans 1:7)*

God the Son:
- *"But unto the Son he saith, Thy throne, O God, is for ever and ever: a sceptre of righteousness is the sceptre of thy kingdom." (Hebrews 1:8)*
- *"...and not after Christ. For in him dwelleth all the fulness of the Godhead bodily." (Colossians 2:8-9)*

God the Holy Spirit:
- *"But Peter said, Ananias, why hath Satan filled thine heart to lie to the Holy Ghost... thou hast not lied unto men, but unto God." (Acts 5:3-4)*
- *"And grieve not the holy Spirit of God, whereby ye are sealed unto the day of redemption." (Ephesians 4:30)*

God the Father

God is a Father to all who come to Him by faith in His Son, Jesus Christ. God excels above all fathers, loving to give good gifts to His children, providing for their needs, teaching and chastening them, and desiring their fellowship. As the first person of the Trinity, He is the Father of the Lord Jesus Christ, having sent Him into the world as a visible representation of Himself.

God the Father in Scripture:
- *"A father of the fatherless, and a judge of the widows, is God in his holy habitation." (Psalm 68:5)*
- *"If ye then, being evil, know how to give good gifts unto your children, how much more shall your Father which is in heaven give good things to them that ask him?" (Matthew 7:11)*
- *"Blessed be God, even the Father of our Lord Jesus Christ,*

the Father of mercies, and the God of all comfort;"
(2 Corinthians 1:3)

- "For whom the Lord loveth he chasteneth, and scourgeth every son whom he receiveth. If ye endure chastening, God dealeth with you as with sons; for what son is he whom the father chasteneth not?" (Hebrews 12:6-7)

Did You Know?

Many structures in nature illustrate well the idea of the Trinity: one being with three components.

- Man is made up of soul, spirit, and body.
- The world is composed of earth, sky, and sea.
- Matter is made up of solids, liquids, and gases.
- Water has three forms: liquid, ice, and steam.
- The egg is made up of the shell, the white, and the yolk.
- Neutrons, protons, and electrons form the atom.

Perhaps one of the clearest examples is found in geometry. For every geometric object there are three dimensions: height, width, and depth. Each of these dimensions is a unique component which can be examined separately; we can study the height of an object apart from its width and depth. However, all three components are necessary to make a whole; to isolate them is to do away with the object. To have width, for example, is to have height and depth.

God reveals Himself through each of the three persons of His Being, with each One evidencing different aspects of the divine character and nature. The Father, Son, and Holy Spirit have different roles, and although they may operate separately, their will and purpose is always one.

God the Son

Jesus Christ is the second person of the Trinity. Although He was *"...made in the likeness of men"* (Philippians 2:7), He has existed eternally and is in every way equal with His Father, God. *"I and my Father are one." (John 10:30)* Through Jesus Christ, God manifested Himself in physical form to all men. This incarnation is spoken of in John's gospel, where the Bible calls Jesus the Word of God. *"In the beginning was the Word, and the Word was with God, and the Word was God. ... And the Word [Jesus] was made flesh, and dwelt among us, (and we beheld his glory, the glory as of the only begotten of the Father,) full of grace and truth." (John 1:1, 14)*

The Scriptures clearly declare Jesus Christ as the Creator and Upholder of all things. Through Him, God created the world. *"...God, who created all things by Jesus Christ." (Ephesians 3:9)* We read further in John 1:3: *"All things were made by him; and without him was not any thing made that was made."* Not only is Christ the Creator, but His word and power hold all things together. *"Who [Jesus Christ] being the*  *brightness of his [God's] glory, and the express image of his person, and upholding all things by the word of his power..." (Hebrews 1:3)* "The universe is neither self-sustaining nor is it forsaken by God... Christ's power causes all things to hold together. The pulses of the universal life are regulated and controlled by the throbbings of the mighty heart of Christ."[3]

Jesus Christ was ordained by God to be the mediator for mankind, and only through Him can men have access to God the Father. It is by faith in God's Son that we find forgiveness for

3. William Evans, *The Great Doctrines of the Bible*, The Moody Bible Institute of Chicago, 1974

sins and receive the gift of eternal life.

- *"For there is one God, and one mediator between God and men, the man Christ Jesus;" (1 Timothy 2:5)*
- *"Jesus saith unto him, I am the way, the truth, and the life: no man cometh unto the Father, but by me." (John 14:6)*
- *"For the wages of sin is death; but the gift of God is eternal life through Jesus Christ our Lord." (Romans 6:23)*

Key Concept

Jesus Christ is God Almighty.

God the Holy Spirit

The Holy Spirit is the third person of the Trinity, as much Almighty God as the Father and the Son. *"God is a Spirit: and they that worship him must worship him in spirit and in truth." (John 4:24)* The Holy Spirit is not merely an influence or power stemming from God, rather He is a Divine Being, existing eternally, with His own role and established works.

Scripture points to the Holy Spirit as co-Creator of the world. The first mention of Him in the Bible is on the opening pages of Genesis, *"...And the Spirit of God moved upon the face of the waters. And God said, Let there be light...." (Genesis 1:2-3)* Job 26:13 records that, *"By his spirit he hath garnished the heavens..."*

The Holy Spirit was sent as a successor to Jesus Christ, taking the place of His physical presence on the earth. Prior to His death, Jesus told His disciples that He would send the Holy Spirit to comfort them and teach them in His absence. *"But the Comforter, which is the Holy Ghost, whom the Father will send in my name, he shall teach you all things, and bring all things to your remembrance, whatsoever I have said unto you." (John 14:26)*

Notable Quote

"The close kinship of Christ with Christianity is one of the distinctive features of the Christian religion. If you take away the name of Buddha from Buddhism and remove the personal revealer entirely from his system; if you take away the personality of Muhammad from Muhammadanism, or the personality of Zoroaster from the religion of the Parsees, the entire doctrine of these religions would still be left intact. Their practical value, such as it is, would not be imperilled or lessened. But take away from Christianity the name and person of Jesus Christ and what have you left? Nothing! The whole substance and strength of the Christian faith centres in Jesus Christ. Without Him there is absolutely nothing."

—Sinclair Patterson

The Bible Explored

The Bible uses many names in reference to the Holy Spirit, giving us insight into His role and character.

- The Spirit of Grace: *"Of how much sorer punishment, suppose ye, shall he be thought worthy, who hath trodden under foot the Son of God, and hath counted the blood of the covenant, wherewith he was sanctified, an unholy thing, and hath done despite unto the Spirit of grace?"* (Hebrews 10:29)

- The Spirit of Truth: *"Howbeit when he, the Spirit of truth, is come, he will guide you into all truth…."* (John 16:13)

- The Spirit of Life: *"For the law of the Spirit of life in Christ Jesus hath made me free from the law of sin and death."* (Romans 8:2)

- The Spirit of Wisdom and Understanding: *"And the spirit of the LORD shall rest upon him, the spirit of wisdom and understanding…."* (Isaiah 11:2)

- The Spirit of Promise: *"… in whom also after that ye believed, ye were sealed with that holy Spirit of promise,"* (Ephesians 1:13)

- The Spirit of Glory: *"If ye be reproached for the name of Christ, happy are ye; for the spirit of glory and of God resteth upon you...."* (1 Peter 4:14)

- The Spirit of God: *"For as many as are led by the Spirit of God, they are the sons of God."* (Romans 8:14)

- The Spirit of Christ: *"...Now if any man have not the Spirit of Christ, he is none of his."* (Romans 8:9)

- The Comforter: *"But when the Comforter is come, whom I will send unto you from the Father, even the Spirit of truth, which proceedeth from the Father, he shall testify of me:"* (John 15:26)

Conclusion

Nowhere does the Bible attempt to prove the existence of God. The Scriptures simply state His existence as fact, proclaiming, *"In the beginning, God..." (Genesis 1:1)* Neither can one find in recorded history an origin for belief in a Sovereign Being; every culture, language and people group from the beginning of time has had Deity inscribed in their very hearts and minds. *"For the invisible things of him from the creation of the world are clearly seen, being understood by the things that are made, even his eternal power and Godhead; so that they are without excuse:" (Romans 1:20)*

The Bible tells us in Psalm 14:1, *"The fool hath said in his heart, There is no God."* In the words of William Evans, "No one but a 'fool' will deny the fact of God. 'What! No God? A watch, and no key for it? A watch with a main-spring broken, and no jeweler to fix it? A watch, and no repair shop? A timecard and a train, and nobody to run it? A lamp lit, and nobody to pour oil in to keep the wick burning? A garden, and no gardener? Flowers, and no florist? Conditions, and no conditioner?' He that sitteth in the heavens shall laugh at such absurd atheism."

God's greatness is beyond our ability to comprehend. He is the Almighty, All-knowing, Ever-present One. He is glorious in holiness, unequaled in His love, unwavering in His justice. Each person of the Godhead is perfectly matched to meet humanity's every need: God the Father, the Provider and Protector; Jesus Christ, the Redeemer and Mediator; the Holy Spirit, a Teacher and Comforter.

The study of God is of paramount importance, influencing our views on every facet of life, including: the world, human relationships, our choice of morals, our duty, and our outlook on eternity. God is the most amazing subject to engage the mind of man. The God of the universe has placed before us an unparalleled opportunity to fellowship closely with Him. As the Scripture so plainly tells us:

DRAW NIGH TO GOD, AND HE WILL DRAW NIGH TO YOU.
JAMES 4:8

GOOD AND EVIL INTERNATIONAL

IN OUR VISION, THE GOOD GUYS WIN.

Good and Evil International forms the base of operations for a unique set of warriors for Christ. We are a Bible-based, missions-focused organization that delivers the saving message of the Gospel of Christ through innovative, technologically savvy media.

Good and Evil International produces and distributes print, electronic, and video versions of the Good and Evil graphic Bible storybook and other communication products. We offer ways for supporters to actively participate in mission opportunities. We have sent over 100,000 books to prisons worldwide; through this outreach, many have come to know the Lord.

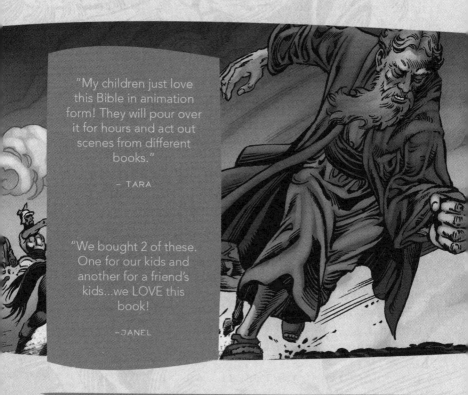

"My children just love this Bible in animation form! They will pour over it for hours and act out scenes from different books."

– TARA

"We bought 2 of these. One for our kids and another for a friend's kids...we LOVE this book!

–JANEL

Before continuing to the next lesson, please answer all the questions in the Q&A section below. If you prefer, you can download a printable Q&A booklet and answer key from our web site:

www.getbiblefirst.com/downloads

1. Complete the following sentence: God is greater in wisdom

   and power than _____

   _____.

2. Fill in the blanks: As the Creator, only God has

   _____, _____

   knowledge of all things.

3. Complete Hebrews 4:13: "Neither is there any creature that

   is not manifest in his sight: but all things are _____

   _____

   _____."

4. According to James 2:19, do satanic hosts acknowledge God's power?

    _____

5. List three things that God cannot do.

    1. _____

    2. _____

    3. _____

6. Fill in the blanks: God's power is never used for _____
    _____; rather it always
    works in accord with His _____
    _____.

7. Is there any place that is exempt from God's presence, perception or awareness?

    _____

8. Complete the sentence: Man, angels, and even Satan are limited by distance and space, but God exists outside the

    _____.

9. Which of God's characteristics do angelic beings constantly proclaim before His throne?

    _____

10. Fill in the blanks: Because God is holy, His very being
    _____ and cannot allow it
    to _____.

11. What does the Bible tells us in I John 4:8?

     _____

12. List three characteristics of God's love:

     1. _____

     2. _____

     3. _____

13. Fill in the blank: God's _____ rewards men equitably according to their works.

14. Complete the sentence: God is the _____ of all mankind, rewarding the _____ for their good deeds and punishing the _____ for their sin.

15. Finish Job 37:23 "Touching the Almighty, we cannot find him out: _____

     _____

     _____."

16. What is the name of the doctrine that teaches One God in Three Persons?

     _____

17. Fill in the Scripture: "_____

     _____, the Father, the Word, and the Holy Ghost: and these three are one." 1 John 5:7

18. The New Testament proclaims: a _____ who is God, a _____ who is God , and a

the middle letter of the whole Hebrew Bible, and made even more detailed calculations than these."[4]

Sir Frederic Kenyon further explains… "These trivialities, as we may rightly consider them, had yet the effect of securing minute attention to the precise transmission of the text; and they are but an excessive manifestation of a respect for the sacred Scripture which in itself deserves nothing but praise. The Massoretes were indeed anxious that not one jot nor tittle, not one smallest letter nor one tiny part of a letter, of the Law should pass away or be lost."[5]

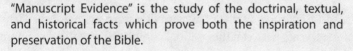

Did You Know?

"Manuscript Evidence" is the study of the doctrinal, textual, and historical facts which prove both the inspiration and preservation of the Bible.

4. F.F. Bruce, *The Books and Parchments, Revised edition*, Westwood: Fleming H. Revell Co., 1963

5. Josh McDowell, *Evidence that Demands a Verdict*, Here's Life Publishers, Inc., San Bernadino, CA 1979

_____ who is God,

each one manifesting the Godhead in all of its _____

_____.

19. Check all that apply to God the Father:
    - ❑ gives gifts to His children
    - ❑ is called the Comforter and teacher
    - ❑ chastens His children
    - ❑ provides for the needs of His children

20. Fill in the blank: The Scriptures clearly declare

    _____ as the Creator and Upholder of all

    things.

21. Through Whom alone do men have access to God the
    Father?

    _____

22. Who is the third person of the Trinity?

    _____

23. Jesus told His disciples that when He left them He would
    send the Holy Spirit to do what?

    _____

    _____

24. What important truth does James 4:8 impart?

    _____

    _____

    _____

Bible First ™

God Created the
Spirit Beings

How to complete this lesson

1. Read the lesson.
As you read, be sure to jot down any comments or questions you have. You'll want to keep your King James Bible handy to look up passages as you progress.

2. Answer the questions.
You'll find these in the Q&A section at the end of the lesson. We recommend that you write your answers in the corresponding Q&A booklet* which you may download from our web site.

3. Check your work.
Once you have completed the Q&A booklet, verify your answers with those found in the answer key* for this lesson.

Studying with a coach?
If you were given this book by a Bible First coach, be sure to let them know once you complete this lesson. That way, you can share your work from the Q&A section and discuss what you've learned before continuing to the next lesson.

*Available at www.getbiblefirst.com/downloads

Lesson Overview

- The Many Kinds of Spirit Beings
- The Power and Limitations of the Angels
- Common Misconceptions About Angels
- Lucifer: God's Anointed Cherub
- The Fall of the Angels
- The Future of the Angels

Introduction

A dedicated student of the Bible soon realizes that an ongoing spiritual war is being fought between the forces of God and the armies of evil. It is clear that beyond our ability to see or comprehend, there exists a spirit realm in which plans are formed, battles waged, petitions made, and which positively or negatively affects the affairs of men.

Many Kinds of Spirit Beings

The Bible refers to many different kinds of spirit beings, clearly defining some as good and others as evil. Many of them differ greatly in physical form and in their work and activities. Some appear on the pages of Scripture frequently, while others are referred to by only a few verses. Those spiritual beings on the side of good serve God and seek to fulfill His purposes. They are referred to by many names and differ amongst themselves.

Angels

Angels are widely referenced in Scripture and generally come to mind the most quickly. The Bible also calls them ministering spirits, sons of God, morning stars, and heavenly host.

- Ministering Spirits: *"Are they not all ministering spirits, sent forth to minister for them who shall be heirs of salvation?" (Hebrews 1:14)*

- Sons of God: *"Now there was a day when the sons of God came to present themselves before the LORD, and Satan came also among them." (Job 1:6)*

- Morning Stars: *"Where wast thou when I laid the foundations of the earth…When the morning stars sang together, and all the sons of God shouted for joy?" (Job 38:4,7)*

- Heavenly Host: *"And suddenly there was with the angel a multitude of the heavenly host praising God, and saying, Glory to God in the highest, and on earth peace, good will toward men." (Luke 2:13-14)*

Angels are often found delivering messages from God to men,

such as when Mary was told by the angel Gabriel that she would be the mother of God's Son. The Bible records that they can appear as ordinary men, and that they have great strength and spiritual power. As messengers of God, the words of angels are steadfast, meaning that what they speak has authority and will come to pass.

One angel, Michael, is given particular mention in Scripture as the archangel, "arch" meaning chief or commander. Michael presides over other angels and is seen leading hosts of angels into battle. (Revelation 12:7) He is also called Daniel's prince and "the great prince" standing on behalf of the nation of Israel. (Daniel 10:21; 12:1)

The Bible mentions a peculiar incident involving Michael: a confrontation with the devil over the body of Moses. *"Yet Michael the archangel, when contending with the devil he disputed about the body of Moses, durst not bring against him a railing accusation, but said, The Lord rebuke thee." (Jude 1:9)*

On this occasion, Michael combatted the devil in a remarkable way. Despite the extraordinary power and wisdom that Michael possesses, the great archangel dared not rely on his own strength to overcome the devil, but countered him with a far mightier weapon: the name of the Lord.

The Bible Says

"Bless the LORD, ye his angels, that excel in strength, that do his commandments, hearkening unto the voice of His word." (Psalm 103:20)

Gabriel is another noteworthy angel mentioned by name in the Bible. He was commissioned on several occasions with miraculous revelations straight from the throne of God. *"...I am Gabriel, that stand in the presence of God; and am sent to speak unto thee, and to shew thee these glad tidings." (Luke 1:19)*

The Old Testament records Gabriel explaining complex

prophetic visions to Daniel about the future of the Israelite people. In a New Testament case, Gabriel was entrusted with the birth announcement of John the Baptist. When Zacharias, the astonished father-to-be, refused to believe the news that his wife would bear a son, Gabriel responded with a swift judgment: Zacharias would not be able to speak until the baby was born. Perhaps the most celebrated tidings delivered by Gabriel were to the virgin Mary, foretelling the birth of God's own Son, Jesus Christ.

Did you know?

The multitude of angels in the heavenly realm is beyond our ability to comprehend. They are so many they cannot be counted.

- *"But ye are come unto mount Sion, and unto the city of the living God, the heavenly Jerusalem, and to an innumerable company of angels." (Hebrews 12:22)*
- *"And I beheld, and I heard the voice of many angels round about the throne and the beasts and the elders: and the number of them was ten thousand times ten thousand, and thousands of thousands." (Revelation 5:11)*

Cherubim

The Old Testament refers to another type of spirit being known as cherubim. Scripture tells us repeatedly that God dwells in the midst of these creatures and that they surround His throne. *"O LORD of hosts, God of Israel, that dwellest between the cherubims..."* (Isaiah 37:16) *"The LORD reigneth; let the people tremble: he sitteth between the cherubims..."* (Psalm 99:1)

The book of Ezekiel portrays the cherubim as some of the most extraordinary and fantastical spirit beings. According to Ezekiel's vision, these magnificent creatures have four faces: that of a man, lion, ox, and eagle. They are described as having two sets of wings: one set is outstretched and joins with those of another cherubim, one set covers their bodies. Their feet are likened to calves' feet and sparkle like highly polished brass. They are luminous creatures that glow with the brightness of fire and reflect the glory surrounding the throne of God. They move with the speed and power of lightning.

"As for the likeness of the living creatures, their appearance was like burning coals of fire, and like the appearance of lamps... And the living creatures ran and returned as the appearance of a flash of lightning... Then the glory of the LORD went up from the cherub... And the sound of the cherubims' wings was heard even to the outer court, as the voice of the Almighty God when he speaketh." (Ezekiel 1:13-14; 10:4-5)

Good and Evil, No Greater Joy Ministries

Seraphim

The spirit beings known as seraphim are only mentioned by name in one passage of Scripture. From the book of Isaiah, we learn that they are six-winged creatures who stand above God's throne, hovering in His presence and declaring His glory.

"...I saw also the Lord sitting upon a throne, high and lifted up, and his train filled the temple. Above it stood the seraphims: each one had six wings; with twain he covered his face, and with twain he covered his feet, and with twain he did fly." (Isaiah 6:1-2)

Apparently, the seraphim's primary purpose is to mightily proclaim the holiness of God. *"And one cried unto another, and said, Holy, holy, holy is the LORD of Hosts: the whole earth is full of his glory."* (Isaiah 6:3) Isaiah reports that their cry was so powerful that the noise of it shook the very door posts of the temple of God.

The Power of Angels

"Bless the LORD, ye his angels, that excel in strength..." (Psalm 103:20) Throughout Scripture, great strength is attributed to angels, and several verses specifically designate them as "mighty angels." (2 Thessalonians 1:7; Revelation 10:1; 18:21) A number of detailed accounts highlight their power and give insight into their nature and capabilities.

In Genesis, two angels visited Lot in the decadent city of Sodom. When the men of Sodom attempted to break down the door and abduct the heavenly visitors, the angels effortlessly smote their attackers with blindness. (Genesis 19:11)

Another account of angelic deliverance is detailed in the book of Daniel. While serving as chief advisor to King Darius of the vast Persian empire, the prophet Daniel was unjustly sentenced to be thrown into a den of lions. The propagators of this evil scheme rejoiced over his certain death at the mouths of these wild and ravenous beasts. To the amazement of all, Daniel emerged unscathed after spending an entire night with the starving lions. Announcing his supernatural protector to be an angel from God, Daniel proclaimed to the king, *"My God hath sent his angel, and hath shut the lions' mouths, that they have not hurt me...."* (Daniel 6:22)

As mentioned before, the angel Gabriel authoritatively silenced Zacharias for his unbelief. *"...I am Gabriel, that stand in the presence of God; and am sent to speak unto thee, and to shew thee these glad tidings. And, behold, thou shalt be dumb, and not able to speak, until the day that these things shall be performed, because thou believest not my words, which shall be fulfilled in their season." (Luke 1:19-20)*

Prophetically, the power of the angels is manifested in the book of Revelation. They are the instruments by which God pours out His wrath on those who have rejected Him. Angels are seen doing such things as causing all manner of plagues on the earth, making severe proclamations of judgment, and even exercising control over the elements.

The Bible Explored

The Scriptures make it evident that our human vantage point is finite; we cannot see or understand all that takes place in the spiritual realm. In regard to heavenly things, the Apostle Paul said, *"For now we see through a glass darkly, but then face to face:..." (I Corinthians 13:12)* We are separated from the spiritual dimension by our mortal bodies. However, the battle between good and evil is raging around us all the time.

The Old Testament gives a fascinating account of the prophet Elisha that illustrates our limited understanding. In the book of II Kings, chapter 6, Israel was being attacked by Syrian forces. Time after time, the Israelites would gain the upper hand because of perfect intel regarding the enemy's location, activity, or strategy. Finally, the king of Syria began to suspect betrayal:

"...Will ye not shew me which of us is for the king of Israel? And one of his servants said, None, my lord, O king: but Elisha, the

prophet that is in Israel, telleth the king of Israel the words that thou speakest in thy bedchamber." (2 Kings 6:11-12)

Elisha the prophet, at God's direction, had been revealing to Israel all the movements of the Syrian army. As soon as the King of Syria was made aware of this, he responded by saying:

"...Go and spy where he [Elisha] is, that I may send and fetch him.... Therefore sent he thither horses, and chariots, and a great host: and they came by night, and compassed the city about." (2 Kings 6:13-14)

Upon waking in the morning, Elisha's servant saw the army laying siege to the city and cried to his master, *"...Alas, my master! how shall we do?" (2 Kings 6:15)* Elisha's answer reveals not only his strong confidence in the power of the Lord his God, but also his insight into the spiritual realm. *"...Fear not: for they that be with us are more than they that be with them. And Elisha prayed, and said, LORD, I pray thee, open his eyes, that he may see. And the LORD opened the eyes of the young man; and he saw: and, behold, the mountain was full of horses and chariots of fire round about Elisha." (2 Kings 6:16-17)*

Like us, the young man could not see the spiritual forces at work all around him, but they were nonetheless present. God went on to smite the Syrian host with blindness and deliver them into the hands of the Israelites.

The Limitations of Angels

Despite the astounding power of the angels, Scripture is clear that they do not possess unlimited authority and abilities. Rather, they are created beings who are subject to limitations and weaknesses. They are not to be deified.

Contrary to many superstitious beliefs and religious practices, angels are not to be worshiped. Angels themselves worship God exclusively. Moreover, they are very careful to protect God's supremacy and ensure that men do not worship them in His place. In the Old Testament, an angel appeared to a man named Manoah to announce the birth of a son. When Manoah and his wife sought to honor the angel by a sacrifice, the angel resolutely responded: *"...if thou wilt offer a burnt offering, thou must offer it unto the LORD...." (Judges 13:16)*

Again, in the closing chapter of Revelation, the Apostle John was overcome by apocalyptical prophecies he had received from an angel, and bowed down to worship the heavenly being. The angel immediately rebuked him. *"...And when I [John] had heard and seen, I fell down to worship before the feet of the angel which shewed me these things. Then saith he unto me, See thou do it not: for I am thy fellowservant, and of thy brethren the prophets, and of them which keep the sayings of this book: worship God." (Revelation 22:8-9)*

Key Concept

Contrary to many superstitious beliefs and religious practices, angels are not to be worshiped.

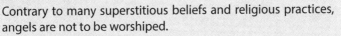

Angels are never given authority to assert their own ideas or revelations. Although they are instrumental in bringing messages from God, they are only channels of those messages, not the originators of them. While many men and women claim to have received special knowledge directly from an angel, if this revelation contradicts the Word of God, it is completely baseless, and its propagator accursed. The apostle Paul said in Galatians 1:8: *"But though we, or an angel from heaven, preach any other gospel unto you than that which we have preached unto you, let him be accursed."* The apostle John adds, *"Beloved, believe not every spirit, but try the spirits whether they are of God: because many false prophets are gone out into the world." (1 John 4:1)*

Unlike God, angels are not all-knowing. The Bible points to several facts about which angels are ignorant. For example, Jesus said that they do not know the time of His coming. *"But of that day and hour knoweth no man, no, not the angels of heaven, but my Father only." (Matthew 24:36)* Furthermore, Peter tells us that although some of the Old Testament prophecies concerning Christ were revealed unto men, angels do not have a full understanding. Like researchers on the brink of discovery, they yearn to know more of God's redemptive plan. *"...which things the angels desire to look into." (1 Peter 1:12)*

In ways similar to man, angels can experience temptation and are able to choose between good and evil. However, unlike men, angels who sin are never shown mercy because they do so with full knowledge of who God is, His glory, and His holiness. They do not walk by faith as men do, but by sight. When they turn their backs on their Creator, they fully comprehend the eternal consequences of choosing evil. Angels who have sinned come under the rule of Satan and are referred to as devils, evil spirits, and unclean spirits.

Common Misconceptions About Angels

In order to have a correct view of angels, it is important to note not only what the Bible says about them, but what it does NOT say. Several prevailing beliefs about angels are actually misconceptions that have no foundation in Scripture.

For example, the Bible never refers to angels or other spirit beings as female. In the instances where they appear on earth, angels are always men. Throughout Scripture, pronouns describing spirit beings are always of the male gender. The only angels named in Scripture bear the male names of Michael, Gabriel, and Lucifer.

Contrary to artists Donatello and Raphael, "putti", or childlike angelic beings are not accurate portrayals of Biblical spirit beings. Figures of babies and toddlers were frequently incorporated into Renaissance and Baroque paintings which depict scenes from the Bible and Biblical personages. "Putti", almost always male, often naked and having wings, have given rise to the belief that children are transformed into angelic creatures at death and now flutter about the heavens. Nowhere is this supported by Scripture.

Furthermore, angels do not have wings. Scripture clearly describes the heavenly creatures cherubim and seraphim as having many (more than two) wings, but angels, God's messengers, are never depicted with wings. In fact, the author of Hebrews states that some people have had angels as guests in their home, not realizing that they were more than ordinary men. *"Be not forgetful to entertain strangers: for thereby some have entertained angels unawares." (Hebrews 13:2)*

Finally, angels are commonly believed to be departed spirits of men. However, the Bible teaches that they are a separate race that was created by God before the foundation of the world. Scripture clearly states that men die once, at which point they either go immediately into the presence of the Lord or else face eternal judgment.

- *"We are confident, I say, and willing rather to be absent from the body, and to be present with the Lord." (2 Corinthians 5:8)*

- *"And as it is appointed unto men once to die, but after this the judgment:" (Hebrews 9:27)*

Lucifer: God's Anointed Cherub

Before the first moments of this world's creation, before the thundering waves of the sea, the structure of the atom or the formation of DNA, God's artistry was already manifest in the splendor of the heavenly creatures. Whether by the sound of God's voice or the touch of His mighty hand, the spirit beings were brought forth: the six-winged, mighty-voiced seraphim to hail His holiness, the swift cherubim with four faces and outstretched wings as the guardians of His throne room, the innumerable host of angels as His messengers and servants, each one known to Him by name. Foremost among all of these unfathomable creatures emerged one, Lucifer, anointed above them all, perfect in beauty, bedecked with gems and gold, full of wisdom, resplendent with brightness, and resounding with celestial melodies to God's glory.

God Himself conferred on Lucifer the lofty position of prince over all the angelic host. He endowed him with talents, beauty, wisdom, and status—everything one could possibly desire. Scripture records God's words regarding this elevated cherub, *"...Thou sealest up the sum, full of wisdom, and perfect in beauty... every precious stone was thy covering... Thou art the anointed cherub that covereth; and I have set thee so: thou wast upon the holy mountain of God... Thou was perfect in thy ways from the day that thou wast created...."* (Ezekiel 28:12-15)

The Bible Says

"Where wast thou when I [God] laid the foundations of the earth...When the morning stars sang together, and all the sons of God shouted for joy?" (Job 38:4,7)

The Bible Explored

The devil did not start out as a wicked deceiver. When God created him as a perfect angelic being, he was called Lucifer, meaning "bringer of light" or "morning star". After his rebellion, the Bible identifies him by two titles: Satan, meaning "adversary" in Hebrew, and the devil, meaning "accuser" in Greek. These two names aptly describe the active role he plays in opposing God and men.

- Adversary: *"Be sober, be vigilant; because your adversary the devil, as a roaring lion, walketh about, seeking whom he may devour:"* (1 Peter 5:8)

- Accuser: *"...for the accuser of our brethren is cast down, which accused them before our God day and night."* (Revelation 12:10)

Lucifer's Rebellion

Regrettably, Lucifer's heart became lifted up with pride. He ceased to be thankful for the magnificent blessings bestowed upon him and disdained the One from Whom they came. Instead of reveling in the goodness of His Creator, Lucifer began to revel in himself. *"Thine heart was lifted up because of thy beauty, thou hast corrupted thy wisdom by reason of thy brightness..." (Ezekiel 28:17)*

In Isaiah 14, God reveals the enormity of Lucifer's ambition: *"For thou [Lucifer] hast said in thine heart, I will ascend into heaven, I will exalt my throne above the stars of God: I will sit also upon the mount of the congregation, in the sides of the north: I will ascend above the heights of the clouds; I will be like the most High." (Isaiah 14:13-14)*

Lucifer, the first to commit sin, attempted to usurp God's position as the ruler of all things. God decidedly crushed his rebellion and cast him out of heaven. *"How art thou fallen from heaven, O Lucifer, son of the morning! how art thou cut down to the ground, which didst weaken the nations!" (Isaiah 14:12)* *"And the great dragon was cast out, that old serpent, called the devil, ... and his angels were cast out with him." (Revelation 12:9)*

Lucifer had a following of angels that sided with him in his rebellion. Stripped of his angelic position, Lucifer became Satan, the devil, the tempter and deceiver of men, the enemy of God and everything good. The angels that fell with him are commonly referred to as demons, but Scripture calls them by many other names, including devils, familiar spirits, unclean spirits, seducing spirits, principalities, powers, and rulers of darkness.

- Devils: *"Thou believest that there is one God; thou doest well: the devils also believe, and tremble."* (James 2:19)

- Familiar Spirits: *"Regard not them that have familiar spirits, neither seek after wizards, to be defiled by them: I am the LORD your God."* (Leviticus 19:31)

- Unclean Spirits: *"And unclean spirits, when they saw him [Jesus], fell down before him, and cried, saying, Thou art the Son of God."* (Mark 3:11)

- Seducing Spirits: *"Now...in the latter times some shall depart from the faith, giving heed to seducing spirits, and doctrines of devils;"* (1 Timothy 4:1)

- Principalities, Powers, and Rulers of Darkness: *"For we wrestle not against flesh and blood, but against principalities, against powers, against the rulers of the darkness of this world, against spiritual wickedness in high places."* (Ephesians 6:12)

The Fate of Satan and His Angels

In just retribution for the immeasurable evil that Satan and his hordes have perpetrated, God has designed a horrible place of judgment. Weeping, wailing, gnashing of teeth, perpetual darkness, and unquenchable torment are all part of this hellish environment; it is called the Lake of Fire. At an appointed time, Satan and his angels will be cast there to suffer for all eternity. *"And the devil that deceived them was cast into the lake of fire and brimstone, where the beast and the false prophet are, and shall be tormented day and night for ever and ever." (Revelation 20:10)* The Bible further refers to, *"... everlasting fire, prepared for the devil and his angels." (Matthew 25:41)* Their judgment will be final and eternal.

The Bible Explored

In our society, Satan and evil spirits have been given increasing attention in films, books, music, games, and even in worship. People from all economic levels and backgrounds have become involved in the occult, witchcraft, palm reading, horoscopes, signs of the zodiac, and other satanic-oriented practices. The Old Testament reveals God's hatred toward these activities:

"There shall not be found among you any one that maketh his son or daughter to pass through the fire, or that useth divination, or an observer of times, or an enchanter, or a witch, or a charmer, or a consulter with familiar spirits, or a wizard, or a necromancer. For all that do these things are an abomination unto the LORD...." *(Deuteronomy 18:10-12)*

Scripture further speaks in a negative light of *"...the astrologers, the stargazers, the monthly prognosticators...".* *(Isaiah 47:13)* Anything relating to the occult or divining the future is part of Satan's realm, and he uses it to draw men away from God. His hateful plan is to entrap as many as possible in his own destruction.

The Bible exhorts us to remain simple concerning evil, and forbids us to have any dealings with the works of darkness.

- *"...yet I would have you wise unto that which is good, and simple concerning evil." (Romans 16:19)*
- *"...let us therefore cast off the works of darkness, and let us put on the armour of light." (Romans 13:12)*
- *"...and I would not that ye should have fellowship with devils. Ye cannot drink the cup of the Lord, and the cup of devils: ye cannot be partakers of the Lord's table, and of the table of devils." (1 Corinthians 10:20-21)*
- *"And have no fellowship with the unfruitful works of darkness, but rather reprove them." (Ephesians 5:11)*

The Bible Says

"Thou art wearied in the multitude of thy counsels. Let now the astrologers, the stargazers, the monthly prognosticators, stand up, and save thee from these things that shall come upon thee. Behold, they shall be as stubble; the fire shall burn them; they shall not deliver themselves from the power of the flame: there shall not be a coal to warm at, nor fire to sit before it." (Isaiah 47:13-14)

Conclusion

The message of the Bible is not just the story of mankind, but an epic of vast proportion, involving the opposing spiritual forces of good and evil. Even before the creation of man we see the beginning of a great war. Lucifer's rebellion commenced the turmoil between good and evil which has spanned the whole earth and encompassed all generations. From cover to cover, the Bible expounds on the efforts of Satan to thwart God's plan. But, the end of this seemingly ageless conflict has already been foretold. The final chapters of Scripture make it clear that this war will culminate with Satan's demise and the exaltation of Jesus Christ over all.

"THAT AT THE NAME OF JESUS EVERY KNEE
SHOULD BOW, OF THINGS IN HEAVEN, AND THINGS
IN EARTH, AND THINGS UNDER THE EARTH;
AND THAT EVERY TONGUE SHOULD CONFESS THAT

JESUS CHRIST IS LORD,

TO THE GLORY OF GOD THE FATHER."

PHILIPPIANS 2:10-11

Before continuing to the next lesson, please answer all the questions in the Q&A section below. If you prefer, you can download a printable Q&A booklet and answer key from our web site:

www.getbiblefirst.com/downloads

Q&A

1. Fill in the blanks: A dedicated student of the Bible soon realizes that an ongoing _____ _____ is being fought between the _____ _____ and the _____ _____.

2. What are four other names that the Bible uses in reference to angels?

   _____

   _____

3. What is the name of the archangel?

   _____

4. What does the term "arch" mean?

   _____

5. In combat with the devil over the body of Moses, what mighty weapon did Michael rely on?

   _____

6. What angel was commissioned with revelations straight from God to men?

   _____

7. What were the most celebrated tidings delivered by Gabriel?

   _____

   _____

8. Which spirit beings surround God's throne and have four faces?

   _____

9. Finish the verse: "As for the likeness of the living creatures, their appearance was like _____ _____, and like the _____...And the living creatures ran and returned as the appearance of a _____..." (Ezekiel 1:13-14)

10. Which spirit beings have six wings and stand above God's throne?

    _____

11. What is the primary purpose of the seraphim?

    _____

_____

12. Complete the verse: "And one cried unto another, and said,

_____

_____." (Isaiah 6:3)

13. What did the two angelic visitors do to the men of Sodom to avoid being abducted?

_____

14. What judgment did Gabriel impose upon Zacharias because of his unbelief?

_____

15. What did Elisha's servant see when the Lord opened his eyes?

_____

16. Fill in the blank: Contrary to many superstitious beliefs and religious practices, angels are not to be

_____.

17. Many men and women have claimed to receive revelation from angels. How can we know if such revelations are true? (choose one)
    ❑ The circumstances were unquestionably supernatural.
    ❑ The Word of God confirms or denies it.
    ❑ The church authorities support it.
    ❑ A great majority of people follow it.

18. Why do angels who have sinned not receive mercy?

_____

_____

_____

19. There are many common misconceptions about angels that have no foundation in Scripture. Mark the following sentences true or false.

- Angels are female. ❑ True ❑ False
- Children are *not* transformed into angels at death.
  ❑ True ❑ False
- Angels do not have wings. ❑ True ❑ False
- Angels are departed spirits of men. ❑ True ❑ False

20. Before man's creation, who was endowed with the lofty position of prince over the entire angelic host?

_____

21. Complete the sentence: Lucifer, the first to commit sin, attempted to _____

_____.

22. After he was cast out of heaven, who did Lucifer become?

_____

23. Define the following names:

- Lucifer: _____
- Satan: _____
- Devil: _____

24. Into what place of torment will God cast Satan and his angels to suffer for all eternity?

    _____

25. Fill in the blanks: Anything relating to the

    _____ or _____

    _____ is part of Satan's realm,

    and he uses it to draw men away from God.

26. What is the foretold end of the seemingly ageless conflict between God and Satan?

    _____

    _____

27. Finish the verse: "That at the name of Jesus _____

    _____, of things in heaven, and

    things in earth, and things under the earth; and that every

    tongue should confess that _____,

    to the glory of God the Father." (Philippians 2:10-11)